Pen Tangle

A Collection Of Poems on the Five Elements

Ruhi Shah

INDIA • SINGAPORE • MALAYSIA

ISBN
Paperback: 979-8-89744-178-5
Hardcase: 979-8-89744-179-2

This book is dedicated to my mother -

a moonchild and healer.

XVIII
THE MOON

Contents

FIRE – 6

WATER – 24

AIR – 42

EARTH – 56

SPIRIT – 74

ABOUT THE AUTHOR – 93

First, there was Fire,

and it consumed all.

XXI
THE WORLD

Cardinal Sin

Lipid pools of espresso, his eyes
is just how I like my coffee.
Fuming dark lava,
or the inside of a coffin.

His fire-starting touch,
is just how I like it,
raw as a burning wound
and ragged as my breath.

Keep It in the Kitchen

We brewed till
it all boiled over.

Our little pot spilt
and marked the stove
with silver rings.

It scarred us
bejewelled
black and blue

We didn't call it love
just a call of distress.

Liber

Scarlet embers sear and hiss
as fumes rise and slither up
I taste the shadow of my
blackened blood.

It isn't sweet as milk,
and there is nothing kind
about charred skin and bones
and yet, only fire can liberate.

Dawn

Over the tomb of treasure
dandelions will make love again.

What is lost will soundly sleep
with rose petals laid still.

When the ego is inflamed
climbing to the truth is a slippery slope.

Thorns will prick
we will keep waking up.

My First and Last

In the beginning,

Fire kindled me gently in the womb.

It was purple, filled with newborn possibilities.

In the end,

Fire consoled my weary body and ready soul.

It was bright white, as the light at the end of the tunnel.

Flamed

Black as beaten coal
red as the setting sun,
blue as my wretched soul.

Many hues you have
and they stay with me
from cradle to the kiln.

Cost of Life

We swing in between
roaring forces
of life and death,
from our very conception
we begin to disintegrate.

Heart to Heart

Peel your sleeves back
and place your heart
in your palms
so we can
exchange
our destinies.
Keep your pennies
in your pockets, deep.
I'm talking about taking
everything you ever wanted.

Gunpowder

These balmy nights
the spirit soars for sable flights

It wants you or someone like you.
or anyone, to paint it bright.

Ashtray full, cups empty
it's the broken flower child
that picks the gun first.

Their hearts lay shot and forsaken,
their minds have gone astray.

The Story

The fire that gives
takes too, it takes two
to cause friction
it takes more
to churn reality
into fiction.

Baptism By Fire

You still run like acid in my veins
under my skin, silent magma sleeps.
It scorches your bitter-cold absence
and in this heat, I am renewed.
Half you and half what was me.

I Shouldn't Have Said Forever

My heart is branded
with our jilted love.

I used to think of you often,
while daydreaming in quaint places.

But now empty halls
whisper your name, too.

Your presence is molten,
moving mountains beneath my feet.

Refugee

Lover, not a fighter
your touch danced like
Virgil's words in Aeneid.

All the catastrophe
became cosmic behaviour.

Let's Meet on Xmas Eve

Candles and stockings

Christmastime snowfall

pillows and smokes,

we had everything going for us

yet we fell prey to disaster

and burned faster than

scented wax.

We Were Both Fire Sign

Can I indulge you with Hennessey?
Can I borrow your tongue, please?
I like your words and how
you twist it, rip it, you say
exactly what I'm thinking.

South shore to northwest
Destiny had to burn its map
to give us a chance.

Long Distance Break-up

Fate can make us dance
but it cannot move the stones
placed upon our hearts.

Why blame the past?
when our knees are too weak
to make the moves last.

Not every lover forsakes the lie
not all stars meet in the sky,
so, let's burn these teary ties.

The siren of the sea sings serenely

Yet her roar can sink

the most hardened soul.

XX
JUDGEMENT

Wine and Dine

Promise me springtime posies
and sangria-soaked sanguine kisses.
Let me lay over you and sink
my lips into your petaled chalice.

Cyclone

Feelings don't come
as waves that play
gently on the shore.

It's a sneaky whirl
coming to swallow
the Captain's pride.

Salt in Our Skin

We ran in giddy waves
to drink the salted ecstasy
of dark, moonly tides.

The sands of yesterday slid off
and we emerged naked;
glistening with hope.

Sunken

Atlantis wasn't made in a day
but it takes one giant wave
to pull down the mighty.
Never lose faith in the humility,
never let a fake cause cause a rumble,
when there is so much at stake
to let it all crumble.

Salt in Your Cologne

Absolve my ache
with your ocean touch
let me flow to the
rhythm of waves.
Your scent of the sea
carries me to infinity.

Call of the Sea

Clouds wept into a creek
but the raindrop's destiny
beckoned it to the Great Sea.

It was halfway to Bliss.

Till a beastly dam
broke its path and held it captive
in its unyielding grey walls.

The pool of prisoned waves
now prays for a catastrophe,
a merciful strike to set blues free.

Sea and the Seeker

In this magnanimity
we are but a dew drop
seeking equanimity.

Understand that knowing is a
heavy hammer punching
our old, pretentious manners.

Only the worthy might
climb over stormy heights
And reach the heart of the sea.

Chasing Oceans

Time dances on one's tongue
moments of sweetness
seem smaller than bitter bites.

We are bound by our reflections
where is the freedom of being
when tied to these phantom chains?

Pleasure or Pain

Gratitude is a nine-letter word
when the four-letter evades me.

The only four-letter I know are
the scars left at your wake.

Longing strikes me at half past midnight.
Half I try to resist
the velvet veil of melancholy.

Over and Under

The ebb caresses and carries light
even in shadows, it harbours hope.

From lucid turquoise shores,
to the dark, dormant depths
life happens where the water flows.

Gut Feelings

I drink intuition
with my morning tea,
it screams you're bad for me,
I ditch it like a garbage bag.

I switch on emotions
with my bedroom light.
it sighs I'm ready for you,
I believe it like the Bible on my nightstand.

Underwater Rites

With every guzzle of storm

flailing current caught my lungs,

unrelenting as a prodigal lover.

Earnest creatures of the shade

carved my mortal name in cursive

on the mossy abyssal grave.

Loop

When the broadcast of the tragic
looms overhead like colourless rainbows
when coffins come in standard issue
and ropes are stored in a convenience store
Death becomes charity.

Boxing Day Circa 2004

If silence was a songbird
she was screeching that dawn,
singing with stolen deities
and sleepy sunken senses.

When the sea returned,
it had the might of an ocean.
and it was greater than the walls
that people built around their hearts.

Crashing as an army of frothy titans
it claimed everything on its way,
retreating only to leave behind
the briny gift of decay.

Prophecies

Revelation is a poison
that makes you sicker
but leaves you stronger.

It's a black horse in tinsel and bells
and chaos is the main character
we are merely the audience to its wrath.

Rebirth

I reincarnated from
The holy water
Made of sweat,
blood and tear
Spent on loving you

Now, when I write
the gods hear.
When my palms go tight
The gates of heaven open
And light pours in.

On its weightless shoulders
the wind carries ponderous bales
In its aimless way, we find reason.

XI
JUSTICE

Arrows Need Faith

It swings the strings to sing a lullaby
and it howls with rage, too.
Every utterance rides on its glorious wings.
The arrow and aim are insignificant
when the wind decides to change direction.

Last Winter

You came as
a silver Palamino
riding the icy winter,
a promise hung from the mistletoe.

Snowflakes clung on
the branches that night,
when passion swayed your voice,
they were both delicate and brittle.

Memoir from Emerald Islands

The mist of the tea rose evokes joy
of opening a manila envelope that
shrines my grandparents' gift.

The taste of betel leaf is as sublime as
the long drives, windows down
when bliss surfs on the sea breeze.

Oud and musk become the portal to devotion,
every dawn and dusk, they linger
as a veil between the worlds.

Our breaths are borrowed.
Truth and love have their home
outside the hourglass.

Spring in Our Steps

We were two kids

Running wild

With no one to stop us

From catching the wind

With our bare hands.

His Baritone is Sacral and Criminal

My heart was struck by lightning
swinging from the throat to the belly.

I grew greedy to be the muse of his music.

If only I could persuade him to play;
the tunes I could not string together.

My tongue was twisted in a tornado.

The Rumble

Reckoning beats its drum
to bring out the realisation.
It wrenches out your heart
from your thumping chest
and places it on the altar,
where the truth sits
ready to greet the red,
dripping and drying with
each passing moment.

Rewind

When your music fills my bedroom
I feel the light even on the nights
the moon goes on holiday
And the stars don't peak
from behind the curtain.

Now that you're gone,
I turn my mind to you early morning
to relive how I woke up next to you.
in your white T-shirt.

Claws and Crown

She was no princess

But a monster uncaged,

In fishnet stockings and satin drapes,

She roared when she broke the golden chains.

Tonight, it's an unholy war

between your icy intentions

and her animal instincts.

Sacred Gaze

The further you went

The deeper I sank into your eyes

They look like shadows at noon.

Between us, there is no space.

It's solid, like mighty, consecrated stones.

Enigma

He raised her veil
But her eyes were closed.
It's the nature of women and stars,
we talk in codes and thrive in clandestine
Never to be tamed, our tresses fall free.

Poet from the Islands

I am the bard under the thatched roof

sipping coconut water and gazing at the shore,

while you were counting city lights and paper planes.

This poem isn't commissioned,

it's a humble submission to the weave of words.

It's an excerpt of my tiny reality; these letters hold my

essence in their curves.

Snuffed Out

The wind has caught flame's wings,
and the candle lies bare now with
just an empty wick and elusive smoke.

The smoke will never
catch up to where the light goes.

She never abandons her babe
But sacrifices him readily
For the sake of higher grounds.

III
THE EMPRESS

Small Town Girls

Bursting heartaches
Beaming smiles
Doleful hope and,
Daring dreams.

We plant our feet in
sparkling sands and salty seas
piercing our ears with pearly clouds
and licking the setting sun upon the azure.

Status Quo

These God-fearing men
Fear them, for they fear none
But the sound of gold coins
Slipping on the glass ceiling.
Then we hear the broken spines
bowing down before the divide.

Eden and Amazon

Shallow shrubs
and patchwork posies
sleep prim and pruned.

Do their fragile petals dream
of breaking the picket fences?

Do they remember
the freedom of the forest?

Awake

Those who hide in the forest of dreams

wake to the glory of blood and gore.

Outside the enchanted bubble, innocents weep,

and the soldiers fight to feed themselves.

Have you ever wondered what is the cost of one life?

It must be nothing more than one's morality.

A Rose, Lotus, and Sunflower Walked Into A...

A rose

guarded by thorns

beckons a stranger

with fragrant passion.

A lotus

meditating on lake

guides the seeker to

reach peace within.

A sunflower

persevers the night

to follow the morning light.

Be My Constant

Lillies may wilt,
a storm may swallow the seeds
but the garden will stay
as a place where possibility blossoms,
even after the dust has settled.

The Gardenia

The lone gardener toils
For the fragrant breeze of
The radiant white bloom
that blossoms in solicitude.
Dew drops of misty morning epiphanies
perch on it and it is guarded by
twirling ivy and sundews.

You Are Rooted in Me

The love for you went deep.

From the crown to within,

twisting around my naval,

down to my core.

It grounded me,

when you were

planted far away.

She Takes What She Gives

Curled up in a celestial cradle
her chest rises and falls,
rises and falls in clockwork.

Most generous is her bosom
yet the stranger awaits
eager for his breathless acolyte.

Auld Lang Syne

I sip venom for the kisses we shared
tip of your tongue becomes my pen
twirling on the paper, deep blue.

Our old conversations fill my ears
it fixes the gap between our hearts
easing my tired, storm-teased soul.

Music sounds like your fingertips
swiftly running across the piano
aching, swirling with secret angst.

Pyramid and the Spinx

That you seek is not in the mines
it's not in gilded watches and diamond rings
metal is not a weapon of mass destruction.

That you seek is not in the cellar
the wine can't patchwork your bleeding soul
the whiskey is not the cure for loneliness.

That you seek is not in the court
justice cannot be bought or sold on scales
the law is alive; she is a lionhearted eagle.

Trickster Grim Reaper

The one who cries with thunder
Has forsaken the lightning.

The nature of death,
is an illuminated passage for the illumined mind,
and a justly fated, unjust sorrow for the rest.

Die every day, won't you?
Die every way, dear lover.

Transcendental

The divine is delicate
as dew drops on a rose
and snowflakes that sink into the skin,
it's the scent of a secret glade
that grows in one's essence.

Funeral Song

What a waste of beauty,
the cruel fate of daisies!
To be plucked and slain
just for adorning
crude flesh and bones.

From Monsoon to Spring

August beckons autumn

with drip-drop sonnets

It will sing till

the leaf goes brittle.

Then soon the winter

will embrace it tight

the leaf will break and beg

for another day in the summer.

Little Joys

The snail inches home
second by second
till the hour dark
kisses its soft trail.

The day slips
hour by hour
Ttll the tangerine sun
brings a new dawn.

The spirit never settles
It keeps seeking, like a fool with
abundance of yearning.

0
THE FOOL

Better Off as Friends

You,

Child of the night

your undying kisses

paints me, gold.

I,

a speck in the midnight sky

craving your uncaring touch

to calm my weary mould.

You're slow to believe in our love,

and my fast mind undone,

was our dopamine hit.

Springtime Confessions

Lucent crescent hung above us
and flame of the forest burned
the velvety spring skies with
incandescent scarlet kisses.

Under this blossoming shade,
I followed the light in your eyes
and traversed the cosmic wild
that is how I became yours.

Intentions

The Conjurer in-between
forms flames from the fire
clouds from the air
waves from the water
And ashes from the heart.

A Date with Anubis

At the crossing of the Great River beyond

A man in a billowing cloak stands soaked

He waits for me, intently gazing

through his beetle black hooded eyes

He holds a parchment with my deeds

And when I reach him, he asks

"From which chalice would you drink?"

Zealous

I ride an adamant chariot.
Ruby, Lapis, Opal, and Jade
are my steeds' names, they fly,
Pegasus over Olympia,
My desires take on mammoth wings
they are as precious as Magnolias in the fall.

Greatness in Us

You, a vessel of clay
with dust in your bones
holding the breath of wisdom
that has walked for aeons.

You, with water in your veins
lame with doubts in your essence
carries the clue to tomorrow
which comes without fail.

Childhood Trauma

When chaos swings the crib
Lullabyes sound like a banshee's screech.

The gale steps in from the window
To lick the baleful purple flame.

The night's shade makes the toy,
Into a teething monster.

Mystic's Love

Know that your arms might
be too short of embracing fully
the mystery of its grand grasp,
yet under its intoxicating influence
your heart can breathe whole.

Sugar

As she swooned to
the endless night
a glee glazed her gaze
the stars swirled her core
like blueberry and vanilla cone
On a balmy summer evening.

Writer's Take

The nib is as big as the universe
and then many folds.
It has placed pharaohs on draft
and trapped angels in small letters.
No hero or villain is more menacing
than an ink blot.
No man is bigger
than his maker.

Infidel

The mayhem of midnight
thrives in clandestinity.

When pious promises of morning descend,
pits of porcelain pearl cradle perversity.

Moonlit perfidy purges all pretence of purity.

Eyes on the Horizon

For those who dream of distant waters
hardly see the rose in their garden
They pine for the other when
Their own needed touch.

Such is the curse to thrust your trust
On a young sailor man.

Witches and Warlocks

What happens to the unseen, the unheard?
I've heard fate is cruel to the unknown
Burned girls of Salem will agree.
And the big-bearded druids often said:
Men only seek answers they like to hear
And kill questions they'd rather not see.

Spirit of Bohemia

Counsel may turn to dust

When wisdom stills the water

And knowing kisses zephyr.

Being blooms in gardens

Where the soul can sing free.

Age of Awakening

The young flame doesn't know
that wisdom comes with
temperance and sacrifice.
when the spirit awakens
all inquisitions fall asleep.

I'm afraid there are no turning pages for me.
Once the ink stains, it seeps right into my soul.

About the Author

Hailing from the idyllic Andaman Islands, Ruhi is a writer, poet, and fashion journalist. She takes delight in reading tarot cards and has been doing it for more than ten years, using it to inspire her writings.

Her influences are varied, from classic poets to modern philosophers, from anthropology to theology and mythology. She attempts to grasp the milieu of the now through keen observations and lived experiences.

VI
THE LOVERS

9 798889 744178 5